THE INEXPLICABLE REDEMPTION OF AGENT G

Qui Nguyen

BROADWAY PLAY PUBLISHING INC
New York
www.broadwayplaypublishing.com
info@broadwayplaypublishing.com

Cover art by Jeremy Arambulo
First printing: November 2012
I S B N: 978-0-88145-534-2

Book design: Marie Donovan
Page make-up: Adobe Indesign
Typeface: Palatino
Printed and bound in the U S A

THE INEXPLICABLE REDEMPTION OF AGENT G received its World Premiere at Incubator Arts Project in New York City on 24 March 2011, produced by Vampire Cowboys (Abby Marcus, Producer) in association with Incubator Arts Project. The cast and creative contributors were as follows:

HUNG... Paco Tolson
RUSSIAN FLIGHT ATTENDANT, DINH, TIEN,
PIMP, GOOKIE MONSTER, DHH .... Jon Hoche
SAN, HUY .... Amy Kim Waschke
MOLLY, ABBY, SEXY WHITE GIRL, WIFE,
PHAM ....Bonnie Sherman
QUI, KHUE .... William Jackson Harper
Backup dancer .... Emily Edwards

Director ....Robert Ross Parker
Scenic & lighting design ....Nick Francone
Costume design .... Jessica Shay
Sound design .... Shane Rettig
Puppet design ....David Valentine
Video design ....Matthew Tennie
Dance choreography ....Jamie Dunn
Fight choreography ..... Qui Nguyen & Adam Scott Mazer
Stage management ....Danielle Buccino

THE INEXPLICABLE REDEMPTION OF AGENT G subsequently had its Off-Broadway premiere at The Beckett Theater @ Theater Row on 7 February 2012, produced by Ma-Yi Theater (Artistic Director, Ralph B Pena; Executive Director, Jorge Z Ortoll; Suzette Porte, Producer) in association with Vampire Cowboys with the same creative contributors. The cast was as follows:

HUNG	Neimah Djourabchi
RUSSIAN FLIGHT ATTENDANT, DINH, TIEN, PIMP, GOOKIE MONSTER, DHH	Jon Hoche
SAN, HUY	Brooke Ishibashi
MOLLY, ABBY, SEXY WHITE GIRL, WIFE, PHAM	Bonnie Sherman
QUI, KHUE	Temar Underwood

CHARACTERS & SETTING

Hung
Qui
San
Molly
Russian Flight Attendant
Sexy White Girl
Huy
Tien
Dinh
Abby
Pimp
Khue
Wife
Pham
Gookie Monster

Vietnam

Dedicated to the real life Hung Tran
and my beautiful wife Abby Marcus.

ACT ONE

Introduction

(Title Card: COMING ATTRACTIONS)

(Video: A Grindhouse'esque trailer for LADY SHAOLIN BOUNCER.*)*

*(*JACKIE LEE, *a Chinese Immigrant, walks down a busy street as cool music plays.)*

VOICEOVER: She came from China.
She has a blackbelt in badass and a penchant for taking down straight up suckahs.
Her name is Jackie Lee, LADY SHAOLIN BOUNCER.

(Title Card: LADY SHAOLIN BOUNCER)

VOICEOVER: And she's on a mission for some sweet-tasting vengeance.

(Cut to JACKIE LEE *hitting someone in the face!)*

(Cut to a theater audience. We see JACKIE's *brother working as an usher.)*

VOICEOVER: Ten years ago, her brother was brutally murdered by a man with a mobile-talking device.

BROTHER: *(With accent)* Please turn offa phone. Show about to begin. Sheh sheh!

(As he's turns away, we see an oversized 80s cellphone come up behind him and smashes him in the back of the head.)

(Cut to her brother on the ground dead in a pool of his own blood.)

VOICEOVER: She's now come to America to find that man and kill him with some extreme kung fu violence.

JACKIE LEE: Kiaaa!

(Cut to montage of people on cells getting killed by JACKIE LEE [by breaking necks, throwing stars, etc])

VOICEOVER: Even if it means killing anyone and everyone who owns a phone in the process.

(Cut to a group of yuppies.)

MAGGIE: Andrea, you're gonna turn off your phone this time, right? I'm really excited about this play and I don't want you to ruin it.

ANDREA: No way, bitch. Especially not for some fucking theatre show. What if one of my peeps wants to text me? That shit would be tragic.

MAGGIE: Andrea, please!

ANDREA: Get your nose out of my clam, man. No one gives a shit about fucking theatre anyways. I mean, besides gay-tards.

(JACKIE appears from around a corner.)

JACKIE LEE: You've offended my family and you've offended the ticket-buying audience.

ANDREA: What? You really want my phone, bitch? Only one way to do that. Let's dance.

(JACKIE LEE attacks the group of yuppies with kung fu and ultra-violently kills them all during the next voiceover.)

VOICEOVER: If the carnage becomes too much or if the danger becomes too real, fire exits are located through the door in which you came in and at the side of the stage. Just follow the signs to your safety. But definitely turn off your cellphones now before the Lady Shaolin

Bouncer bounces into your town and kicks the shit out of you.

JACKIE LEE: KIAAAAAAAAAAA!!!

(Abrupt cut to Video Title Card: FEATURE PRESENTATION*)*

(Projection: THE INEXPLICABLE REDEMPTION OF AGENT G*)*

(Projection: Somewhere in the jungle)

(Music like the Rolling Stones Paint it Black *begins playing. We see* HUNG TRAN *appear with a rice hat and a knife.)*

*(*HUNG *is infiltrating a Viet Cong camp and systematically assassinates them one by one.)*

(After taking a handful out in a series of covert moves, he slips up and an alarm sounds.)

*(*HUNG *now finds himself in a gun-fight with an armada of Viet Cong soldiers. However, his superior marksmanship takes them all out one by one.)*

(Cornered with the enemy slowly approaching, HUNG *heaves a grenade at the Viet Cong soldiers which blows them all up in a multi-media explosion!)*

(He poses as the audience cheers wildly.)

1

*(*HUNG *turns to the audience as a single spotlight falls on him.)*

HUNG: Hi, I'm Hung Tran and I'm a badass. I know karate. And I'm Vietnamese...you can tell by my rice hat.

(As HUNG *does this monologue, girls come out and redress his attire from super soldier to something more appropriate.)*

HUNG: And what you are about to see is all completely true. And as we all know, true stories wet your vaginas and get your dicks hard. True stories are awesome!

(The two girls begin making out.)

HUNG: Speaking of truth, this by the way is the third attempt by playwright Qui Nguyen to tell this exact story. He's Vietnamese. Just like me. And though he's written two other plays on this subject, TRIAL BY WATER and BLOOD IN AMERICA, he's never appeared in any of them.
Until now...

(QUI suddenly appears [intentionally played by an African-American actor]. He's tied up with a black sack covering his head. A guard stands beside him.)

QUI: Yo, what the fuck?

HUNG: This time we're gonna play this diddy a little different.

QUI: The hell am I doing here?

HUNG: You're here to help turn this story out correct, playwright.
Ladies and Gentlemen, I give you...Qui Nguyen.

(The guards pulls off QUI's hood.)

QUI: Turn what out correctly?

HUNG: The Gook Story Trilogy.

QUI: Hey man, you can't do this!

HUNG: But I am. How's that for awesome?

QUI: Seriously, I haven't touched this story in years. None of these people have even seen the first two plays, why in the hell would they want to see how it ends. This is fucking weird, man. Playwrights don't appear in their own plays!

(HUNG *signals to the guard. The guard slugs* QUI *in the face.*)

HUNG: Have you ever seen Yellowface?

QUI: Okay, well...that's David Henry Hwang. He's famous and shit. An icon. He represents something. I don't.

HUNG: Oh, but you do.

QUI: No, motherfucker, I don't.

HUNG: Qui, you represent something very important in this story. You represent you.

QUI: I represent me?

HUNG: Yes. You represent you.

QUI: That's fucking retarded.

HUNG: You represent—

QUI: RETARDED!

HUNG: May I continue?

QUI: RE. TARD. ED!!!!

(*The guard slaps* QUI *to the ground.*)

HUNG: You represent the missing piece in a fictionalized tale that with your addition transforms this play from something purely artistic into something truthful.

QUI: Hung, there's nothing truthful about this. This conversation right here—right now—ain't even real. And honestly, dragging me into this is making me come off as some sort of pretentious artsy fartsy SON OF A DICK.

HUNG: Sit here.

QUI: No.

(*The bodyguard looks at* QUI.)

QUI: HEY! I ain't scared of you. You tall overgrown—

(The bodyguard grabs QUI *by the nipple and forces him to sit down as* QUI *screams.)*

QUI: *(Recovering)* Yo, stay the fuck away from me!

(The bodyguard steps towards QUI.*)*

QUI: Come on now!

HUNG: Qui, you've commandeered my life to get Off-Broadway productions. To create a career. You've made money off of some my life's worst tragedies in your previous work and I have never complained or even attempted to stop you. You owe me this.

QUI: That's not fair.

HUNG: You borrowed my life, I'm now commandeering yours to help explain the stories which you've told. You're gonna tell this story right.

QUI: How?

HUNG: That's not my call. That's yours. How are you gonna finish this?

QUI: Hung, I write action-adventure comedies now. COMEDIES! I don't know how to do this. I do shows about ninjas and zombies and b-boys, not boatpeople. YO, FUCK THIS! *(He begins to leave...)*

HUNG: Okay, fine. Go ahead.

QUI: What? You're not going to stop me?

HUNG: If you leave, Qui, I leave.

QUI: I don't care.

HUNG: Really? This is how you wanna leave this? This is how you want your family's story to be remembered?

This is how you want *my* story to be remembered?

HUNG: This is your last chance.

So what's it gonna be, playwright?

(Pause)

HUNG: Alright, let's go, guys. No show here!

QUI: Wait.

HUNG: Don't forget the cheap props.

QUI: WAIT!

(Pause)

QUI: Projection: 1998.

HUNG: What was that?

QUI: It begins with a projection. 1998. It's ten years after you escaped Vietnam.

HUNG: Okay!

QUI: We're in Ho Chi Minh City, Vietnam. Lights come up on a young Vietnamese girl named San.

HUNG: Who's San?

QUI: She's the daughter of Tien, the man you killed on your way to America. But she doesn't know any of that. She's writing you a letter.

(Lights come up on SAN.)

SAN: Dear Hung, My name is San Ngo—

QUI: A Gook Story Part 3: The Inexplicable Redemption of Agent G.

SAN: My father was Tien Ngo. He was on the boat that brought you to the Philippines. I believe he looked after you during your voyage. Perhaps you never spoke to him—perhaps you never had the chance to meet him, but I know he cared for you. If you did meet him, I'm sure you know he was a good man and, like yourself, believed in great ideals. Either way, I know in my heart my father was your guardian angel. I know this because your mother told me this.

I'm sure you have questions regarding your parents as
I have questions about the fate of my father. I feel you
and I have much to share in this matter. I think we can
help each other heal.

Hung Tran, I pray that one day we can finally meet.

Yours truly,

San Ngo

2

(*As* SAN *finishes, lights come up on* HUNG *seated on a plane
reading the letter.*)

(MOLLY *enters holding a shitload of bags.*)

MOLLY: HELLOOO!

HUNG: Oh, hey.

MOLLY: Um, some help here would be helpful.

HUNG: You know what? Maybe we should just stay on
the plane; see where it lands next.

MOLLY: What?

HUNG: I've just been thinking—

MOLLY: You've been thinking, have you?

HUNG: Yeah, maybe I did rush into this—maybe you're
right—it is a bad idea going off looking for this girl—I
mean we don't know if she actually exists. This could
be a con job for all we know. My people are known for
being shifty. Molly?

MOLLY: Oh the fuck no. You're getting off this plane
right now.

HUNG: But—

MOLLY: No. No fucking "but's". You know when a
good time to have cold feet would have been? Twenty-
seven hours ago when we were still in America. No,

strike that, how about two weeks ago before we spent
all our honeymoon money on this fucking trip.

HUNG: So you're not so keen on this idea?

MOLLY: NO! Hung, seriously, come on. You're the one
who wanted come here before our wedding, so if I'm
gonna to have to have an early honeymoon, I want to
start it now.

HUNG: I just ...

MOLLY: What?

HUNG: Nothing.

(Silence)

MOLLY: Look, baby, I get it, okay? You're freaked out.

HUNG: I'm not just freaked out.

MOLLY: You're scared.

MOLLY: Look, there's nothing outside of this plane
that's gonna get you. You're safe. The days of running
away from the Viet Cong are long behind you. You're
an American now. You have me.

HUNG: I know, but—

MOLLY: No, you're not listening. You. Have. Me.

(MOLLY leans down and gives HUNG a kiss.)

MOLLY: Now get your ass moving. They will
eventually want their plane back.

HUNG: Okay.

MOLLY: That's what I like to hear.
And don't worry, baby, if those pesky Viet Cong
actually do show up—which I'm planning on—we're
gonna kill the shit out of those fucking commie
bastards.

HUNG: Whatchoo talking about, White girl?

MOLLY: Why do you think I packed three suitcases of sweet spy gear and karate weapons with us? It's not a vacation unless there's some explosions, right?

HUNG: *(To* QUI*)* Qui, what the fuck is this?

QUI: *(Suddenly appearing)* Telling it the way I want to fucking tell it. Or did you forget? This is a Qui Nguyen show, bitch.

(A male RUSSIAN FLIGHT ATTENDANT *enters.)*

RUSSIAN FLIGHT ATTENDANT: Vould you like more drink please?

HUNG: A Russian flight attendant on a Vietnamese airline?

MOLLY: It's a communist spy!

(The RUSSIAN FLIGHT ATTENDANT *pulls out a gun.* MOLLY *kills him.)*

MOLLY: So we gonna do this, baby?

HUNG: Let's go kick some yellow booty.

3

(A SEXY WHITE GIRL *takes an old fashioned mic and talks all sexy in it.)*

SEXY WHITE GIRL: *(Sexily)* And now, for all you naughty boys and girls joining our story late, a quick recap of the first two plays in A GOOK STORY TRILOGY.

Previously on TRIAL BY WATER: A GOOK STORY PART ONE...

HUY: *(With a bad Asian accent)* Oh, big brother Hung, I so sad. Our parents have placed us on this small fishing boat to escape Vietnam, but unfortunately because we are so poor they could not afford to come with us. I miss them so bad.

HUNG: *(Also with a bad Asian accent)* Don'ta worry, little brother Huy, we having each other. I protect you. Our mother and father may be dead now because they wanting to stay and fight communist Vietnam, but we will be safe because we having each other.

HUY: What if the Viet Cong are on this boat, big brother Hung? What if they finding out we are the fifteen and thirteen year old sons of Khue Tran, an underground South Vietnamese freedom fighter who they are in search for? They will surely kill us.

HUNG: Don'ta worry, Huy. No one here on this boat know anything about us. We are completely safe.

TIEN: *(An equally bad Asian accent)* Herro! My name is Tien, I am secret South Vietnamese freedom fighter who knowing both your mother and father.

HUNG & HUY: OH NO!

TIEN: Don'ta worry. You mommy and daddy sent me here to helping you!

HUY: Should we trust him, big brother Hung?

HUNG: No, little brother Huy. Father telling us to not talk to any strangers.

TIEN: But I not a stranger. I am Tien, a secret South Vietnamese freedom fighter who knowing both your mother and father.

HUNG: Thank you, but we not needing your help. This trip only taking one week. We can handle taking care of ourselves for one week. There going to be no problem at all.

TIEN: Oh, we'll see. We'll see.

SEXY WHITE GIRL: However, the engine dies, stranding the two young and virile Vietnamese boys out in the middle of the hot and sweaty China Sea without any food or water. Later in the play . . .

HUY: Oh, big brother Hung. I so hungry. We have been on this boat for almost three week now. All our food and water have run out and now the other passengers are resorting to killing and eating the weaker passengers for food. What are we going to do?

TIEN: Herro, rittle boys! It is I, Tien, secret South Vietnamese freedom fighter who knowing both your mother and father. Are you hungry? I can helping you. Here is bag of carved up flesh I took from a passenger I *killed*. You want it? Tastes like chicken!

HUNG: No way. I Buddhist which means I'm a vegetarian which means I do not eat meat which definitely means eating human flesh would be a very very big no-no.

TIEN: FINE. YOU DON'T WANT MY HELP? I DON'T WANT TO HELP YOU ANYMORE.

HUNG: Who say we wanting your help?

TIEN: Oh. Then maybe I helping you DIE instead.

HUNG: What?

TIEN: I just kidding! Jokes, kid, jokes! Well...maybe.

SEXY WHITE GIRL: Look at me. I'm hot. Are you hot? Do you know what else is hot? The China Sea. Later in the play...

HUNG: Rittle brother Huy! Rittle brother Huy! Where are you?

TIEN: Herro, it is I, Tien, secret South Vietnamese freedom fighter who knowing both your mother and father.
So maybe you wanting my help now?

HUNG: I needing nothing from you.

TIEN: Oh, your little brother say same thing. Now rookie at where he is.

HUNG: What you mean?

TIEN: I seeing our brother. He floating dead out at sea. Rook!

HUNG: Oh no! What happened?

TIEN: Well, don't rookie at me. I don't know. But I am sure he did not get killed and eaten by group of cannibalistic passengers that was led by me. Oh no. That is definitely not what happened.

HUNG: I feel so bad.

TIEN: You should. But what are you going to do, huh? Maybe you should just go and join him. Have a nice day!

SEXY WHITE GIRL: Do you know what's nice? Being bad. Do you want to see something really bad. Do you want to see something really really bad? Do you want to see someone tied up? I do. Cause I'm a bad little devil, just like Hung.

HUNG: Wake up, Tien.

TIEN: Why you having a knife? You going to kill me?

HUNG: Yes. That's why I tied you up in your sleep and have this knife pointed at you.

TIEN: Why? Is it because you found out that I was lying to you and indeed killed your brother and ate his body so I could emotionally torment you?

HUNG: No.

TIEN: Then why?

HUNG: Because I gone crazy!

TIEN: Oh no.

HUNG: And I not just going to kill you, Tien. I going to eat you first. And you are going to watching me.

TIEN: What? But I thought you Buddhist?

HUNG: Not anymore.

(A song like The Talking Head's Psycho Killer *begins playing and* HUNG *kills and devours* TIEN *as the actors playing* MOLLY *and* SAN *appear and do an elaborate Cannibal dance number as* HUNG *kills and devours* TIEN.*)*

TIEN: AAAAAAGH!!!!

*(*SEXY WHITE GIRL *appears on a video screen.)*

SEXY WHITE GIRL: *(On video)* Naughty naughty! Talk about a flesh party! OH MY!
Now for you further enjoyment, you little perverts,
BLOOD IN AMERICA: A GOOK STORY PART TWO...

HUNG: Rook, I finally made it to America. And I'm a rittle ress crazy than before.

MOLLY: *(With a stereotypical southern accent)* Hi, I'm Molly. I'm a simple southern girl who once got raped by my father when I was much younger, but now I'm pretty well adjusted cause he's in jail and I'm bestfriends with the only two Vietna-nese people in town, Tong Tran and Quang Tran, who happen to be Hung's aunt and cousin, respectively. Because of my particularly painful past, I now can relate to young Vietnamese refugees who have gone through traumatic journeys to America. Hopefully I meet one!

HUNG: Hi, I'm Hung. I'm a Vietnamese refugee.

MOLLY: Hi, I'm Molly. I'm an Arkansaw-sian.

HUNG: Let's be friends.

MOLLY: Okay.

(They begin heavily making out and fall behind a set piece.)

SEXY WHITE GIRL: End of plays.

And now we return you to THE INEXPLICABLE
REDEMPTION OF AGENT G: A GOOK STORY PART
THREE...

4

ENGLISH NARRATOR: *(V O)* Lights shift as the stage
transforms into the bustling streets of Ho Chi Minh
City.
Bicyclers wearing pointy rice hats clog the roads as
Hung and Molly fight their way to their hotel.
We see small quaint Vietnamese shops, old Vietnamese
ladies selling Vietnamese flowers, Vietnamese noodles,
and homemade Vietnamese foods.
The streets are filled with commerce including a few
unlucky Vietnamese whores hugging the corners as
they try to entice rich Vietnamese Johns.

WHORES: Me rove you wrong time!

ENGLISH NARRATOR: *(V O)* There is an old Vietnamese
man playing a one string Vietnamese guitar as we see a
slew of other Vietnamese do Vietnamese things under
some Vietnamese paper lanterns.

ALL: THIS IS VIETNAM!

HUNG: *(Breaking character)* Qui, what the fuck is this!?!

QUI: *(Suddenly appearing)* It's a description of Vietnam.
Clearly.

HUNG: Just because you wrote down Vietnam a dozen
times doesn't actually make it Vietnam.

QUI: Well, that's what Vietnam looks like.

HUNG: That's what Vietnam looks like?

QUI: *(Indicating the set which is in this moment just a giant
word VIETNAM)* Yes, motherfucker, can you not read?

HUNG: Have you ever been to Vietnam?

QUI: I don't see how that matters.

HUNG: You've never been to Vietnam, have you?

QUI: Not. Recently.

HUNG: When was the last time?

QUI: Well, if you include my adolescence and the trips we took when I was just an infant...I guess...zero.

HUNG: What?

QUI: It's not that big of a deal.

HUNG: You are writing a play that's central theme is about a young man returning to his home of Vietnam after a ten year absence and you don't see how that matters?

QUI: Well, I've never been attacked by a zombie or flown in outer space, but I've written plays about those subjects. You don't have to actually go through an experience just to be able to write about it. If that was the case, there'd be no such thing as sci-fi.

HUNG: Is this a sci-fi play, Qui?

QUI: No. It's clearly a...spy play?

HUNG: What?

QUI: Nothing!

HUNG: Regardless, I think this is a completely different thing than your "zombie play". Wouldn't you agree?

QUI: It's called research, Hung. Research. I can research it to make it happen.

HUNG: Have you done research?

QUI: Of course. Check this shit out...

MOLLY: Hung, oh my God! Look!

HUNG: What is it, Molly?

MOLLY: It's Ho Chi Minh City, the largest city in
Vietnam which is located near the Mekong Delta. It has
a population of approximately nine million citizens,
making it not only the biggest city in Vietnam, but of
all Indochina. The original name of the city, of course,
was Saigon while it was the capitol of the independent
South Vietnam until its fall in 1975 to the North
Vietnamese during the country's civil war. The name
was changed to Ho Chi Minh City after the conquering
North Vietnamese leader. Citizens however regularly
still refer to this city as Saigon in defiance.

QUI: You've just been wikipedia'd, bitch!

MOLLY: It's quite a sight, isn't it?

HUNG: Yeah. I guess.

MOLLY: Who knew there'd be so many American
chains here already! I've never seen anything like it.

HUNG: Me neither.

MOLLY: This doesn't make you feel weird, does it?
Seeing all this again. It can be a shock. You're okay,
right?

HUNG: Yeah.

MOLLY: Holy shit! Is that a K F Cs?

HUNG: Let's just go find our guide, baby. He's
supposed to be—

(A guide enters.)

HUNG: Right here.

DINH: *(Spoken very slowly) Gum. Ong. Hung. Gum. Ong.
Mee Molly. Em Dinh.*

HUNG: *(Equally slow) Gum. Ong.*

DINH: *(To MOLLY) Em noy Viet?*

MOLLY: *(Like a turtle) Noy Viet Yoy. Hung noy em.*

HUNG: *Molly noy thing mee. Hung noy Viet yoy. Dinh noy thing Mee?*

DINH: *Dinh noy thing mee yoy!*

MOLLY: *Yo ying! Molly noy Viet yoy! Hung noy thing mee.*

HUNG: *Mee?*

DINH: *Mee?*

(All three characters turn and glare at the playwright.)

QUI: What?

HUNG: The hell are we saying?

QUI: It's Vietnamese.

HUNG: A translation would be helpful.

QUI: It's...well, you know. You're saying Vietnamese stuff. In Vietnamese.

HUNG: ...

QUI: Okay, okay. I can't speak Vietnamese either. But this is theatre. I don't have to know Vietnamese to be able to communicate that you two are speaking in Vietnamese because I am fluent in the language of art.

(Ding!)

MOLLY: This doesn't make you feel weird, does it? Seeing all this again. It can be a shock. You're okay, right?

HUNG: Yeah.

MOLLY: Holy shit! Is that a K F Cs?

HUNG: Let's just go find our guide, baby. He's supposed to be—

(A guide enters.)

HUNG: Right here.

DINH: Ching chong ching chong, Hung, ching chong ching chong!

HUNG: Ching chong ching chong travel guide? Ching chong ching chong.

DINH: Ching chong ching chong yes ching chong ching chong. *(To* MOLLY*)* Ching chong ching chong you speak ching chong, White lady?

MOLLY: Ching. CHONG!

DINH: Ching chong awesome!

MOLLY: Ching chong I KNOW!

DINH & MOLLY: Ching chong!

HUNG: Qui. Seriously?

QUI: Shut up. It was a first draft. Here we go:

(Ding!)

MOLLY: This doesn't make you feel weird, does it? Seeing all this again. It can be a shock. You're okay, right?

HUNG: Yeah.

MOLLY: Holy shit! Is that a K F Cs?

HUNG: Let's just go find our guide, baby. He's supposed to be—

(A guide enters.)

HUNG: Right here.

DINH: *(With realistic Asian accent)* What is happening, my brother? You looking for hook-up in this town?

HUNG: Um, I'm actually waiting for a guide.

DINH: You looking at number one guide of all of Saigon, slick. I being your main man.

HUNG: You?

DINH: I Dinh. But friend calling me English because my English is so sweet. I came here because you hiring me from travel agency.

HUNG: You're my guide?

DINH: Can you dig it, suckah?

MOLLY: Why does he keep talking like that?

HUNG: Why are you talking like that?

DINH: To making you feel more like home, my Vietnamese brother and cracker white sister.

HUNG: Who taught you to speak like this?

DINH: From Dolemite movies, motherfucker.

HUNG: Great.

DINH: You sticking with me, Jack, and you won't needing Vietnamese at all. Follow me.

MOLLY: This should be fun.

DINH: Shut up, cracka!

(HUNG, MOLLY, *and the tour guide exit.*)

5

SEXY WHITE GIRL: And now...
A conversation between the playwright and his baby's mama regarding the first draft of this play.

(SEXY WHITE GIRL *puts on glasses and immediately turns into* ABBY *reading a manuscript.* QUI *paces quietly watching her.*)

QUI: So what do you think?

ABBY: What do I think?

QUI: Of the script.

ABBY: It's...um...are you hungry? I'm feeling a bit hungry. Wanna go grab some food? I'm getting a bit light-headed.

QUI: Abby.

ABBY: So...do you wanna go and make another baby?
(She starts doing a seductive dance.)

QUI: Abby.

ABBY: Aw, come on, Qui! You're just gonna get mad
and storm off...

QUI: No, I'm not.

ABBY: Right.

QUI: I'm not.

ABBY: You're sure?

QUI: Yes.

ABBY: It was...well...okay, I guess?

QUI: It was just okay?

ABBY: It was interesting.

QUI: Oh my god! *(He storms off and locks himself into a
different room.)*

ABBY: *(Talking through a door)* I mean...look, maybe I
just have to see it. Alot of plays aren't particularly good
reads at all, but still are excellent plays. As they say,
plays are meant to be performed, not read.

(Pause)

ABBY: It just doesn't sound like you, okay?

QUI: *(O S)* It doesn't sound like me?

ABBY: Your voice. It feels absent in all of it.

QUI: *(O S)* My voice?

ABBY: There's nothing fun about it. There's nothing
outside of the box.

QUI: *(Re-entering)* It's the final play of a trilogy that
I've been working on for over ten years based on my
cousin's journey to America. It's not supposed to be
fun.

ABBY: I thought it was supposed to be about your family.

QUI: It is.

ABBY: Then how come you're not in it? Or your grandmother for that matter?

QUI: This isn't about me. Or her.

ABBY: Actually, I thought it was.

QUI: I get it. You don't like it.

ABBY: It's not a matter about me liking it. I'm just saying... this doesn't feel very "Vampire Cowboys-esque" at all.

QUI: Vampire Cowboys-esque?

SAN: *(As a cheery Japanese television host)* MOSHI, *MOSHI!!!* Fun fact: Qui Nguyen is a co-founder and Co-Artistic Director of Vampire Cowboys Theatre Company of New York City, an Obie Award-winning geek theatre company specializing in creating comic book styled theatrical shows that are filled with martial arts, badass ladies, physically weaker male characters who tend to need saving, and sudden and abrupt genre shifts.

(Someone suddenly pops up with a gun pointed at the Japanese host, she knocks him out while laughing.)

SAN: *(Throwing a peace sign)* Sayonara! Hee hee hee!

ABBY: It just doesn't feel like any of your other plays.

QUI: "Like my other plays?" Did you not just hear the random Japanese girl who just appeared in our living room? You want this to feel like my other plays? It should have what? More kung fu? Sex jokes? Girl-fights? You're missing girl-fights.

ABBY: Baby, I just want you to write a play that makes you feel like you're the one writing it.

QUI: "Like I'm the one writing it?" What the hell does that mean?

ABBY: I'm just saying the other two plays in this trilogy—

QUI: No one else wrote the other two plays. I did.

ABBY: Did you now?
Cue a group of Qui's former playwriting instructors. GO!

(A group of college professors enter.)

HUNG: You can't write the play this way, it would make no sense.

DINH: The original story has no dramatic arc.

SAN: You're serious about putting a joke right here? A joke?

HUNG: You need to restructure everything.

DINH: Your play needs a theatrical device.

HUNG: There's too many characters.

SAN: Overall, it needs to be more Vietnamese.

HUNG: It needs to have Vietnamese in it.

DINH: You should cut all this and rewrite that.

SAN: But not that way!

HUNG: Or that way.

DINH: This is how you should write it.

SAN: To make it more Asian.

HUNG: We shouldn't forget it's Asian.

SAN: Because you are Asian. That's how you got into graduate school in the first place, isn't it? Because you're Asian.

DINH, HUNG & SAN: Make it more Asian!

(The group of college professors make chinky eyes at QUI.*)*

6

SEXY WHITE GIRL: *(On video)* Now my naughty little horn dogs, let's return you back to the streets of Vietnam where our hero Hung explores the streets of Saigon for the first time since childhood. Let's see what kind of trouble he gets into. Hopefully it'll be of the sweaty variety. Mmmm.

(Lights come up as HUNG *walks down the city streets of Ho Chi Minh City.)*

HUNG: *(To himself)* I'm perfectly fine out here by myself, right? This is just like America...just minus the freedom.

There's no Viet Cong here. No, there's no Viet Cong out here. Just normal average ordinary third world malnourished Vietnamese people. It's completely safe to sit here and read my paper...which is completely in Vietnamese...which I can't read at all.

Hm. Maybe I'll just take in the sights.

(To music like Junior Kickstart *by The Go! Team, ninjas suddenly attack* HUNG. HUNG *tries to runs away from them. In the end, however, he ends up fighting them and winning.)*

(He unmasks one of the ninjas. It's the travel guide.)

HUNG: English?

DINH: Can you dig it, suckah!!!

*(*DINH *sucker punches* HUNG *and runs off.)*

(Cut to...)

*(*HUNG *limps back into his hotel room. The scene suddenly becomes film noir.)*

MOLLY: *(Film Noir'ish)* Baby, what's happened to you?

HUNG: *(Film Noir'ish)* I got jumped by three Viet Cong ninjas, one of which was our goddamn travel guide.

(MOLLY *opens a first aid kit and starts dressing his wounds.)*

MOLLY: This is all getting too dangerous.

HUNG: Or maybe not dangerous enough.

MOLLY: You have to stop this, baby! It's just gonna get you killed.

HUNG: Not when we're this close to finding out the score. It's been years, Molly. Ten years and I've never known the score. Do you have any idea what that's like?
My parents died here while I was on a boat headed to America. I've spent years trying to convince myself that not knowing how they died was okay. That not knowing the final fate of my own mother and father would be alright. And just as I was coming around to almost believing that idea, this goddamn letter pops into my inbox and suddenly shifts the paradigm. This girl knows. She has answers. And I'm meaning to find them.

MOLLY: Are you sure that's something you really want, baby?

HUNG: What?

MOLLY: Answers.

HUNG: Don't be a stupid broad.

MOLLY: Baby, I don't mean to throw a wrench, but are you sure this is what you want? How's knowing how your parents died gonna change anything? Ain't it enough that they pulled off the big hit by scoring you a life?

HUNG: No, Molly, it's not enough.

MOLLY: And what are you gonna tell that girl, huh? She's gonna want answers from you too.

HUNG: I'm gonna tell her the truth. I whacked her old man cause he whacked my brother.

MOLLY: Killing her father wasn't enough, was it? Now you wanna hurt his daughter as well. Let the girl have some peace.

HUNG: I thought you were supposed to help me.

MOLLY: And I thought you were done with being fucking crazy. *(She slaps him.)* I'll be in bed.

HUNG: I just need to go get some air.

MOLLY: Don't be out too late.

(Immediate cut to—)

7

(A Vietnamese whorehouse)

PIMP: Herro, how are you? I Vietnamese pimp. You in Vietnamese whorehouse. I have many Vietnamese whores for you to choose from. Very pretty with rots of stamina!

WHORES: Me rove you wrong time.

HUNG: I'm actually just looking for a girl.

PIMP: You needing girl. I have many girl for you! I have fat girl, small girl, young girl, old girl, girl who letting you do whatever you wanting to her—

HUNG: Shut up, creep, that's not what I mean. I'm looking for a specific girl.

PIMP: If you want it, I sure we having it.

HUNG: I'm looking for a girl named San Ngo. I got a letter from her. The return goes to this address right here.

PIMP: What is name again?

HUNG: San. San Ngo. Do you know her?

PIMP: Yes. Yes, I know her.

HUNG: Where is she?

PIMP: You wanting to sleep with the cleaning girl?

HUNG: The cleaning girl?

PIMP: Housekeeper.

HUNG: Get her here.

PIMP: Yes.
SAN! I needing you. Right now. Hurry please!

(SAN, a very attractive—a very seductively dressed woman enters. Think Jessica Rabbit.)

(Music begins playing. The following song is to Katy Perry's Kalifornia Gurls)

SAN: *(Singing)* I know a place

Where freedom's almost over
Sad, sick, and poor
I wouldn't drink the water
Sippin' Lichi juice
Layin' underneath bamboo roofs (undone)
Viet Cong
Break our necks
if we talk about freedom (at all)

You could travel the world
But nothing comes close
To the South East Coast
Once you party with us
You'll be falling in love
Oooooh oh oooooh

Oriental girls
We're inscrutable
Communists
With rice hats on top
Golden skin
So smooth
We'll eat your big Egg roll
Oooooh oh oooooh

Oriental gurls
We're inscrutable
Sly, slick, smart,
We like it on top
Far East represent
Now get your toes bound
Oooooh oh oooooh

PIMP: *(Rapping)*
Sad, poor,
Thin and hungry
She's all yours for a bit of money
V C Eastcoast
These are the hoes you'll love the most
I mean they're cheap
like dirt ass cheap
Fuck her
Smack her
See her weep (huh!)

The girl's so fly
love you long time,
work your wang all night
She's okay
Loves to play
You can fuck all day
She's your yella slave
anal play
and sucking
maybe some finger fucking?

Americans
BANGING gooks
All my girls
FUCKING you
MISOGYNY, SODOMY, ALL ODDITIES
OKAY with me
take two or three
CAUSE you know they BE—

SAN: *(Singing)*
Oriental girls
We're inscrutable
Communists
With rice hats on top
Golden skin
So smooth
We'll eat your big Egg roll
Ooooh oh oooooh

Oriental gurls
We're inscrutable
Sly, slick, smart,
We like it on top
Far East represent
Now get your toes bound
Ooooh oh oooooh

PIMP: Have fun. *(He exits.)*

SAN: *(Femme Fatale-ish)*
Who are you, stranger?

HUNG: The son of Pham and Khue Tran.

SAN: What?

HUNG: You sent me this letter, right?

SAN: You're Hung?

HUNG: In more ways than one, sweetheart.

SAN: Mmmm, that's good to hear.

HUNG: Cool off, I got a lady.

SAN: You do, do ya?

HUNG: That's right. A crispy little cracker that likes Asian spice.

SAN: Interesting.

HUNG: You got info about my parents. I need it.

SAN: So you think you can just come here for a quickie, is that it?

HUNG: I'm here to trade some intel.

SAN: Did you meet my father on the boat?

HUNG: We shared words.

SAN: What kinda words?

HUNG: Uh-huh. I'm not showing my hand until you show me yours. What do you know about my folks?

SAN: Your mom and I were close.

HUNG: How close?

SAN: It was ten years ago...
The night my father left.

(Ten years ago. The following sequence is played out in shadow play. Style-wise, the following sequence is done like an old western.)

SAN: There was a strange wind in the air. A smell that reeked of deception and despair.
Your father called. Told my father there had been a leak. Said someone went to the Viet Cong and gave up the goods on their operation. It was time to book. He told my father—

KHUE: *(Growl-y, like Eastwood)* Someone gave up the goods on the operation. We've been compromised It's time to book.

TIEN: *(Also old Western-y)* What?

KHUE: The Viet Cong knows about us, Tien. They're coming. I'm sending my boys away. To America. There's a boat heading to the Philippines tonight.

TIEN: Wait. You're not going with them?

KHUE: Someone has to draw fire away from those boats.

TIEN: Khue—

KHUE: That's why I called you here, Tien. The V C don't got any goods on you. You can go with my kids and take care of them.

TIEN: What about my family?

KHUE: Pham and I will make sure your wife and daughter are safe. Will you do this for me, Tien?

TIEN: I'm your man.

(In shadow, we see TIEN *mount a horse and ride off.)*

SAN: My mother didn't take the news so well.

WIFE: Heavens be, what do you mean you're going? Going where?

TIEN: I'll send for you and San.

WIFE: You're my husband, Tien, not just one of Khue's posse.

(The light source pans back revealing that TIEN *isn't riding a horse, but instead is having sex with his* WIFE.*)*

TIEN: If I stay, we're all in jeopardy. If I go, we're all safe. We'll be together again, I swear.

WIFE: Tien, please don't.

TIEN: I'm sorry. I have to go.

SAN: As soon as my father left, my mother cried for two straight days. On the third, she took a vile of acid and drank it.

(We see the silhouette of TIEN's WIFE *drink acid and die.)*

SAN: Your parents found me crying over her body. They took me up to the mountains. They tried to hide me. However, the Viet Cong caught up. They found us and brought your father out to a field. He never returned.

(In silhouette, we see KHUE *getting executed.)*

HUNG: And my mom?

(The cowboy facade drops after this, it all becomes very real.)

SAN: She wept. She wept for weeks as I tried to take care of her. One morning, though, the crying just stopped and she was gone.
I pray for them every year, Hung. I mourned for them because I knew you couldn't. You didn't know.
I lost my home. Worked on the street selling anything I could to make a dime. And then I finally found myself back here in Saigon again. Working as a housekeeper. But you should know this—I never sold my body. Not once. No matter how hungry I felt, no matter how much I wanted to find comfort—I never compromised that.

HUNG: I don't need to know.

SAN: Yes, you do.

HUNG: No. You took care of my mom and pop. That's all I needed to know.

SAN: No, there's one more thing.

HUNG: What that?

SAN: Your mother's last words to me. She said—

(We see the ghostly image of PHAM *speaking to* SAN *and* HUNG.)*

PHAM: San, I'm so sorry I cannot be a mother to you. I'm sorry I don't have the strength to be any more

help to you or anyone anymore. My life is lost. I am
done. But you, San, you still have a chance. You may
be sad right now, but there is hope. I want to give you
something.
Find my eldest son, Hung. I know in my heart he is
alive. He made it to America. Find him. And he will
marry you.

HUNG: WHAT!?!

PHAM: He will bring you to America and save you. I
promise you this. My son will be your husband.

SAN: That's right, Tiger. I think you just hit the jackpot.

8

ABBY: Uh, Qui?

QUI: Yes, Abby?

ABBY: Why is Hung's fiance white?

QUI: I'm assuming because of her lack of skin pigment.

ABBY: That's not what I mean. I mean...who the fuck is
Molly?
The real-life Hung Tran is engaged to a Vietnamese-
American girl named Tracy. Why isn't this girl Tracy?

QUI: Oh. That.

ABBY: Yeah.

QUI: Because she's based on Hung's first real-life
girlfriend, Molly, who I introduced in the second play
of the trilogy.

ABBY: Okay?

QUI: So thusly I didn't want to have to add a slew
of new characters for this final chapter of the story.
We already met her previously and I didn't want to
complicate matters by adding yet another character

in which we had to drop a bunch of new exposition to introduce. It's classic Joseph Campbell's Hero's Journey structure.

I mean, what would *Return of the Jedi* be if instead of having Han, Leia, Chewy, and the droids, Lukas would have dropped in a whole different crew of rebels to fight alongside Luke. It woulda been weird.

ABBY: There were the Ewoks.

QUI: Yeah, and the Ewoks fuckin' sucked. Tracy would have basically been an Ewok and I didn't want Hung to be in love with a fuckin' Ewok.

ABBY: Oh, okay. So that's why you made Hung's fiance white.

QUI: For good storytelling.

ABBY: And this whole time I thought it was because you had a white girl fetish.

QUI: Ahem. Say what?

ABBY: That's what the cast thinks, right?

HUNG, SAN, TIEN: *(Adlibbing)* Yeah, totally, absolutetly...

ABBY: I mean you are married to me for instance.

QUI: You Jewish.

ABBY: Jews are pretty white.

QUI: I don't see how this matters.

ABBY: Well, speaking as a whitie, I gotta say...I think your play might be a little...racist.

QUI: Against whom?

ABBY: Asians.

QUI: What? The chinky accents and the ching chong ching chong dialogue? That offends you?

ABBY: Oh, no. That's hysterical. No, I'm talking about the character of San. That bitch is racist.

QUI: She's the daughter of the man Hung murdered. How's that racist?

ABBY: Your depiction of Asian women is that they work in whorehouses looking to marry someone to get to America. For freedom. That's "Miss Saigon", Mister.

QUI: She's not a whore. That's something different.

ABBY: She's been poor her whole life with zero parental guidance and we're supposed to believe she never sold her body for a sandwich.

QUI: Yeah.

ABBY: That's racist.

QUI: Now how's that racist?

ABBY: The other stereotype of Asian women in major media besides being Vietnamese street hookers is that of the virginal innocent schoolgirl. Hello! "The Karate Kid Part Two"! You're just trading one mass stereotype for the other.
I love you, baby, but you're racist.

QUI: I'm not racist.

ABBY: Have you ever dated an Asian girl?

QUI: Why does that matter?

ABBY: Because Qui, I think down deep...you're a white guy.

QUI: Oh fuck no!

ABBY: I'm just sayin'.

QUI: I'm not fucking white!

ABBY: Oh, and one more thing...the use of film noir and shadow play and old western accents right now is pretty fucking strange.

QUI: You think that's strange?

ABBY: Yeah. A little bit.

QUI: You want strange? I'll give ya fuckin' strange.

(Cut to...)

9

(Lights immediately pop up on a thuggish HUNG *lighting a bong. He's dressed all gangsta now.)*

HUNG: *(Gangsta)* What's the big fuckin' deal? I just went out for a hot second. Step off my nuts, yo!

MOLLY: You went to a fuckin' whorehouse, fool, without me. You don't see how that's a problem?

HUNG: Oh, you wanted to go meet some hoes? Is that it?

MOLLY: Don't be raising your voice at me, motherfuckah. I'll cut your dick, I swear.

HUNG: Look, baby doll, I didn't know the place was for slinging tang. I just followed the addy. It led me there. It ain't like I was looking for it.

MOLLY: So did you talk to her?

HUNG: Yeah.

MOLLY: And what she spit?

HUNG: She dropped me the lowdown on what happened to my moms and pops.

MOLLY: And...

HUNG: They died.

MOLLY: That's it?

HUNG: Yeah. What else you think she was gonna tell me? That my mom promised me off to her as a husband or some shit?

MOLLY: No. That's crazy. Why would something like that cross my mind.

HUNG: Oh, cause—funny story. That's exactly what my moms did.

MOLLY: What?

HUNG: Yeah, it's fucked up.

MOLLY: Wow, poor girl. She loses everything, ends up in a whorehouse, and now finds out that the one hope she got to becoming American is gone cause the man she got promised to already got himself tied.

HUNG: Yeah, about that...

MOLLY: What?

HUNG: Well, we ain't exactly married just yet. And that girl is po'.

MOLLY: What are you saying, Hung?

HUNG: I'm saying—you ain't seen her, Molly. Bitch is poor. And when I say poor, I don't mean Arkansas trailer trash poor. I'm talking third world, flies flying around your mouth poor. She's sad. She gots problems.

MOLLY: You ain't serious.

HUNG: All I'm saying is I ain't sure just yet.

MOLLY: What?

HUNG: Yeah, that's what I'm saying. I'm saying...it could go either way from this point. It could go either way.

END OF ACT ONE

ACT TWO

(The following is done as a cutesy "animated digital short")

ENGLISH NARRATOR: And now, a real-life email sent to Qui Nguyen during the world premiere run of TRIAL BY WATER from one of his adoring fans...

SAN: Dear Qui Nguyen, My name is—

(BEEP!!!)

SAN: As you can tell by my name, I am of Vietnamese descent. I came to see your production of TRIAL BY WATER this past Saturday with my aunt. First off, as a member of the Vietnamese American community, I'd like to commend you for doing what you're doing. There is not very much, if any, Vietnamese representation in the world of entertainment and it is inspiring to see someone with the last name Nguyen be able to make a noise in such a competitive arena. It's good to see someone with your talent and background in this profession.

My aunt, like your cousin Hung, was also a refugee. She escaped Vietnam in the early eighties and made it to Hong Kong before settling here in New York. When we saw that you had a new play being produced about this subject, we were both very excited to see what you would do with it.

Unfortunately, the play was awful. Absolutely atrocious. And shockingly quite offensive. We were not very happy with the outcome at all.

You clearly have talent as a writer, Mister Nguyen, but it was heartbreaking to see it used to paint Vietnamese as savages and monsters. You made our people seem evil and petty. I know your play is based on true facts, but was it necessary to make them all cannibals? Was there no other way to show their desperation besides showing their depravity?

We came to the show in hopes to finally see a Vietnamese writer take on a Vietnamese subject and give a different perspective than the evil stereotypes regularly shown in Hollywood blockbusters and Rambo films. However, your play did nothing to dispel those stereotypes. If anything, you helped reinforce them. We left with our heads down and the inability to speak.

It was sad to see such talent wasted on such a horrible horrible play.

Sincerely...

(BEEP!!!)

ENGLISH NARRATOR: And now, part two to THE INEXPLICABLE REDEMPTION OF AGENT G: A GOOK STORY PART THREE...

1

SEXY WHITE GIRL: Lights up on an absolutely realistic depiction of a day in the life of playwright Qui Nguyen.

(QUI enters reading the letter from the angry audience member.)

QUI: "It was sad to see such talent wasted on such a horrible horrible play."
Holy shit.
I'm like the worst Asian ever.

(From behind a short wall pops out GOOKIE MONSTER, *a muppet-style puppet that's clearly a rip-off of the Sesame Street character.)*

GOOKIE MONSTER: Whaddup, my chigga.

QUI: Hey there, Gookie Monster.

GOOKIE MONSTER: You look like someone just punched you in the dick. What's wrong, son?

QUI: I'm reading this letter from an angry audience member about one of my plays. They don't like the way I depicted Asians in it.

GOOKIE MONSTER: Well, let's not lie to ourselves, you do suck at being Asian.

QUI: What?

GOOKIE MONSTER: I know white boys more Oriental than you, son. They study Buddhism, take karate, play video games, date Asian bitches. Do you do any of that stuff?

QUI: No. But I'm actually Asian.

GOOKIE MONSTER: Yeah, technically speaking.

QUI: The fuck does that mean?

GOOKIE MONSTER: Have you looked at yourself recently? You're about as Asian as Michael Jackson is black.

QUI: Dude, Michael Jackson's dead.

GOOKIE MONSTER: Yeah, and if he was truly a brotha, he'd be releasing like ten more albums right about now just like Tupac and Biggie, but no, that bitch ain't done shit. He's dead like Elvis is dead. He's white boy dead.

QUI: Do you have a point in any of this?

GOOKIE MONSTER: The reason why your Asian sister ain't digging your Asian play is cause your Asian play ain't Gookie enough.

QUI: Gookie? What's Gookie?

GOOKIE MONSTER: Yo, you don't know what Gookie is?

QUI: I just thought it was your first name, Gookie Monster.

GOOKIE MONSTER: No wonder you're getting hate mail. Step back, my chigga, let me drop some knowledge on your dumb ass.

QUI: Knowledge in what?

GOOKIE MONSTER: On being Gookie, bitch. *(To the booth)* Drop me a beat!

(A beat is indeed dropped. As it does, the small puppet transforms into a human-sized one.)

GOOKIE MONSTER:
Welcome to gookie monster's rap martial art
Gonna school ya like a buddha, make ya Asian-smart
Perhaps your yella factor is less than par
Gonna flip from a twinkie to a yella supahstar

First things a'goin'
To get your asian flowin'
Is dropping all your instincts
About the things you think
Stink
About being chinky
Don't bring that shit near me
Hear me
Clearly
This be my theory
On what makes ya weary
To answer your query
Lemme speak clearly

Cause ya see plainly
I be
The one and only fresh Gookie Monsta
The monsta who wants ta

Raise yo' self esteem
On being Vetnamese
Cause this be the shit
That's gonna help you with
Become a legitimate
Asian who knows his shit

(HUNG and SAN appear.)

HUNG & SAN: G is for Gookie
That's good enough for me
G is for Gookie
That's good enough for me
G is for Gookie
That's good enough for me

GOOKIE MONSTER:
Oh Gookie Gookie Gookie Starts with G

HUNG: Lemme give assist
We're the Asian hotness—yella actress—
Who'll define this—
More pointed-ly
Than he
So you can see
Exactly—more in factly—
What this word means.

SAN: Moshi moshi motherfucker
Here we go
Gonna flow info
Raise yo' asian ego
So you know in yo' soul
Who yo bros and those who know the pain that we've
all gone through

HUNG: Listen closely—

SAN: It not about minorities or majorities
Or the shit ya see so damn literally

It's more'n skin deep—it's culturely
The shit that binds we—to one another

HUNG & SAN: Makin' us brothas

HUNG: So listen up tight—here's some insight—to
what gookies like—

SAN: Are ya ready?

HUNG: To feel me—feel me—

SAN: Nice!

HUNG: Gookies like—

SAN: Honda Civies, good grades,
Hot ladies, getting paid,

HUNG: Karaoke, Tiger Balm,
Academics, mahjong!

SAN: Uniqlo, Asian pride,
I pimped my car, ain't it fly?

HUNG: Being gangsta, K-town—

SAN: Remove yo shoes

GOOKIE MONSTER, HUNG & SAN: Ya in my house!

SAN: Adding bling to our phones,
Looking young when we're old,

HUNG: Geek chic, arriving late,
Our girls be hot, please don't hate

SAN: Bubble tea, Nintendo Wii,
Noodle shops, Bruce Lee

HUNG & SAN: Jollibee, Pinkberry,
all this shit be gookie!

G is for gookie
That's good enough for me
G is for gookie
That's good enough for me

G is for gookie
That's good enough for me

GOOKIE MONSTER:
Oh gookie gookie gookie starts with G

(Dance break!)

HUNG & SAN: G is for gookie
That's good enough for me
G is for gookie
That's good enough for me
G is for gookie
That's good enough for me

GOOKIE MONSTER:
Oh gookie gookie gookie starts with G

ALL: Oh gookie gookie gookie starts with G

*(*HUNG *and* SAN *immediately disappear as the song ends.)*

QUI: Oh, wow! I didn't realize so much stuff was
Gookie.

GOOKIE MONSTER: That's right, my chigga! What do
you think of that?

QUI: Yeah...
I'm not into any of that shit.

GOOKIE MONSTER: What?

QUI: Yeah, to hell with all that noise.

GOOKIE MONSTER: But what about the angry audience
member?

QUI: Oh. Her?
Yeah, she can go fuck herself.
I'm gonna go grab me a cheeseburger.
Yo, is that Gookie? No? OH—THE FUCK—WELL! *(He
rips up the letter and drops it on* GOOKIE MONSTER*)* Hey,
look!

"I MAKE IT RAIN—I MAKE RAIN—I MAKE IT RAIN
ON THEM HOES! I MAKE RAIN..."
See ya around, Gookie Monster!
Now GET BACK TO WORK!!!

2

QUI: Here we go! Back in Vietnam. Cue motorcycle
riding music!

(Cool motorcycle music begins playing.)

(In a slo-mo action sequence, we see HUNG *and* MOLLY
riding a motorcycle through the country side of Vietnam.)

(Suddenly, MOLLY *spots a ninja on a motorcycle chasing
them.)*

*(Still in slo-motion, they get into a high speed chase and gun
fight.)*

(Finally, MOLLY *leaps from their bike and tackles the ninja.)*

*(*HUNG *stops to see if* MOLLY *is okay. She raises off the
ground slowly.)*

(Suddenly the ninja leaps to their feet, MOLLY *shoots the
ninja in the face.)*

*(*HUNG *runs over to hug* MOLLY. MOLLY *raises a hand
and—)*

MOLLY: Wait just a fucking minute! We're not done
talking yet.

HUNG: Baby.

MOLLY: So did you tell her about her father?

HUNG: Not yet. Hey, don't look at me like that. How
was I gonna bring that up after what she told me about
my parents?

MOLLY: You aren't seriously contemplating marrying
her.

HUNG: It's not like that. It's just—you know—if I can make amends by helping her get to America and out of this shit hole, maybe I should do it.

MOLLY: Maybe she won't want your help once you tell her the truth.

HUNG: Hey, weren't you the one pushing me NOT to tell her about her dad? What's with the change of heart?

MOLLY: What can I say? I'm a selfish bitch. Some girl wants up on my man, I play dirty.

HUNG: My mom promised her that I'd help her out.

MOLLY: Then buy her a car. Don't fuckin' marry her.

HUNG: It's complex, baby.

MOLLY: Not really. Tell her the truth, Hung. Tell her what you did.

HUNG: She'll hate me.

MOLLY: That's her right. You got what you wanted. Give her what she wants.

(Suddenly two ninja jump out and grab MOLLY*!)*

DINH: Ching chong ching chong I got the White Girl Ching Chong!

MOLLY: Hung! Help!

HUNG: Hey, let her go!

DINH: Ching Chong I don't think so Ching Chong.

SAN: Ching Chong yeah we brought some weapons of our own Ching Chong.

DINH: Ching chong we're ready to finish this ching chong.

HUNG: How?

DINH: Ching chong by the only way that matters here in the streets of Vietnam Ching chong.

SAN: By dance battle. Ching. Chong.

(DINH *drops down a boombox.* SAN *lays down some cardboard.*)

(*Music hits.*)

HUNG: Let's do this!

(*A badass beat drops.*)

(DINH *and* SAN *look at each other and then together throw together an impressive pop/lock routine that makes the audience's jaws drop. To finish it off, they hit a big blow-up move and hop to their feet waiting to see how* HUNG *and* MOLLY *will respond.*)

(HUNG *and* MOLLY *pull out guns and shoot the shit out of* DINH *and* SAN.)

(HUNG *and* MOLLY *look at each other.*)

HUNG: I love you, baby.

MOLLY: I love you too!

HUNG: Now come over here with your fine ass. Let me show you how much I love you.

(HUNG *and* MOLLY *suddenly start making-out!*)

MOLLY: Wait, I just need to know one thing.

HUNG: What's that?

MOLLY: You're not attracted to her, right?

HUNG: What?

MOLLY: You're not attracted to her.

HUNG: What? No. She's ugly.

MOLLY: Really?

HUNG: Yeah. Totally. Like so gross.

MOLLY: Give me some sugar.

*(They begin kissing some more. Isaac Hayes begins playing
in the background as* HUNG *and* MOLLY *begin making sweet
sweet love right there on the streets.)*

*(*QUI *interrupts.)*

3

QUI: Psst. So how's the play going?

HUNG: Dude, I'm a little busy here.

QUI: What was up with that dance battle?

HUNG: What?

QUI: The dance battle? Why'd you do that?

HUNG: I don't know—you wrote it.

QUI: I did?

HUNG: Seriously, can we talk about this later?

MOLLY: The mood's totally dead. I'm out.

HUNG: Wait.

QUI: So how's the story?

HUNG: I hate you.

QUI: It's moving alright, right?

HUNG: I don't understand what's up with the ninjas
continually attacking us, but whatevs.

QUI: Ninjas are attacking you?

HUNG: Yeah.

QUI: Shit, I must be mixing up my drafts with one of
my screenplays. Jesus Christ! Why can't I just get this
thing fucking done?

HUNG: I thought you had this trilogy outlined since
you were in grad school.

QUI: I did. I do. It's just doesn't feel like anything anymore.

HUNG: Then maybe you should just—

QUI: Wait, what the fuck am I doing discussing this with you? You're the reason all this shit is happening in the first place. Fuck you.

(QUI *starts to storm off.*)

HUNG: Uh, quick question.

QUI: What?

HUNG: Um, this. This is how you see yourself, playwright?

QUI: What?

HUNG: I've been meaning to say something ever since you stepped onto stage. But this—this is how you see yourself?

QUI: I don't know what you mean.

HUNG: Do you have a little bit more soul here than you do in real life? You know—a bit more hip? A little more "athletic"?

QUI: I'm also a professional fight director.

HUNG: And you're black?

QUI: I was born and raised in a primarily middle-class African-American neighborhood in El Dorado, Arkansas.

HUNG: And that makes you black?

QUI: This is what my heart looks like. And in my heart—in my heart—I'm black.

HUNG: Really?

QUI: *Okay*, so I may not *exactly* look like this, but I'm embodying the spirit of how people perceive my profession.

HUNG: Oh, so this is about your profession.

QUI: Yeah. Playwrights are fucking hot.

HUNG: Oh. Is that right?

QUI: Yeah, that's right.

HUNG: I don't know what world you're living in, but playwrights aren't known for their sex appeal.

QUI: No? Would you like to take a poll?

HUNG: And how are we supposed to do that?

MOLLY: Playwrights are so hot.

SAN: Playwrights make me wet.

TIEN: I'd fuck the hell out of a playwright. That includes you, Qui Nguyen. That includes you.

MOLLY, SAN, & TIEN: GO PLAYWRIGHTS!!!

QUI: Oh. I guess you're wrong, Hung. I am hot.

HUNG: You made them say that.

QUI: You can believe what you wanna believe. I'm the shit.

HUNG: Then how come you don't believe that.

QUI: You don't know what I believe.

HUNG: Then why does this play, as you said, not "feel like anything anymore"? Why do all the plays in this trilogy feel like nothing?

QUI: Go away.

HUNG: I'm just trying to help.

QUI: I don't need your fucking help. I just gotta try harder, that's all. Get to work.

4

(Lights come up on HUNG *and* MOLLY *entering a Vietnamese whorehouse.)*

MOLLY: So this is it?

HUNG: Yeah.

MOLLY: She works here as a cleaning lady?

HUNG: Yeah.

MOLLY: I'd hate to see what she has to clean up.

PIMP: Herro! I Vietnamese pimp. This is Vietnamese whorehouse. How can I be helping— *(Dropping the accent)* Oh. It's you again.

HUNG: Can I speak to San?

PIMP: Look, buddy, this is a business here. If you're not here to buy something, then maybe you should go somewhere else. We don't appreciate window shoppers.

MOLLY: Why don't you just shove it, creep? We just want to talk to—

PIMP: Why hello there. Where did you come from?

MOLLY: I'm with him.

PIMP: Ever thought about modeling, baby. I could use some vanilla on my oriental spice rack.

MOLLY: What?

PIMP: You're absolutely delicious.

MOLLY: Uh, Hung?

HUNG: Look, buddy, I just wanna talk to—

(SAN enters and runs up and hugs HUNG.)

SAN: Hung! You're back!
I knew you'd come back.

MOLLY: Whoa, wait just a minute. That's San. She's San?

PIMP: Yep. That's my cleaning lady.

MOLLY: I thought she was ugly. Hung told me she was ugly.

PIMP: She's Asian. Ain't no such thing as an ugly Asian lady. (*He exits.*)

MOLLY: Hey, keep your hands off of him!

SAN: Who is this?

HUNG: This is my fiancée.

SAN: Oh. Hello.

MOLLY: Yeah, nice to meet you too. Hung, can I have a word with you?

HUNG: Sure. What's up?

MOLLY: That girl is hot.

HUNG: What girl?

MOLLY: That girl.

HUNG: San? Oh, I guess. If you're into that sorta thing.

MOLLY: And what sorta thing is that? Hot girls?

HUNG: Look, it doesn't matter. I'm not attracted to her. Besides, this isn't about attraction. It's about the truth. I'm here to tell her the truth.
So if you don't mind, I have some truth to tell.
San?

SAN: Yes, Hung.

HUNG: I haven't been completely honest with you. I did meet your father.

SAN: You did?

HUNG: Yeah. He was on the boat with me that brought me to the Philippines. The engine died and we were stranded at sea for over a month. People starved to death and your dad...well, he went fucking crazy. He killed my little brother. So I killed him. And then I ate him. Raw. He was completely conscious as I devoured every bit of him. And he watched me. It was gross. I mean really fucking gross. Imagine Rush Limbaugh naked. Yeah, it was even grosser than that. I gagged alot. But I ate every bit of him just like my mom taught me to do at the dinner table. Bit by bit. He tasted a bit like chicken.

SAN: Uh...I don't know what to say...

HUNG: Excuse me... *(To* QUI*)* Playwright?

QUI: Yeah?

HUNG: What the fuck was that?

QUI: I'm trying, okay? Just trying something different.

HUNG: And that is?

QUI: You'll see.

HUNG: Alright. *(To* SAN*)* So I killed and cannibalized your father. It was awful.
Um, so are we cool?

SAN: You murdered my father?

MOLLY: I'm guessing you don't want to marry him anymore, right?

SAN: No.

MOLLY: Awesome. That's all I wanted to know. Let's go, Hung.

HUNG: I'm really very sorry.

SAN: No.
Now you *must* marry me.

MOLLY: What?

HUNG: What?

(Lights shift into a dark red ambiance.)

SAN: *(Like an evil dragon lady)* You killed my father. Now you must make amends for that offence or you shall die.

HUNG: Or I shall what?

(SAN knocks down HUNG with her dragon-lady powers!)

SAN: You really thought I'd just let you go? How foolish! *(To MOLLY)* White girl. You can leave us now.

MOLLY: No.

SAN: Crossing me would not be a very wise plan, white girl. I'm mad powerful.

MOLLY: Oh, I plan on doing way worse than just crossing you, bitch. No one enslaves my boyfriend.

SAN: So you wish to dance, white girl? Then let's dance.

(MOLLY suddenly rips off her clothes revealing a skintight jumpsuit reminiscent of The Bride from The Kill Bill movies or Trinity from The Matrix.)

(SAN pulls out a katana. MOLLY pulls out a katana of her own. They flourish their blades and point them to each other. They circle.)

(Suddenly they attack! The fight is flashy, fast, and awesome.)

(SAN looks like she is about to win but is then suddenly killed by MOLLY!)

(MOLLY turns to HUNG.)

MOLLY: Weaker male character more commonly found in a Qui Nguyen play, take my hand. Now that we've defeated this bitch, there's only one last thing to do.

HUNG: And what's that?

MOLLY: It's time to save the goddamn universe!

(HUNG *and* MOLLY *look up as U F Os enter.*)

MOLLY: Fucking aliens.

HUNG: You're my hero, Molly.

MOLLY: *(Like Bruce Campbell)* Yeah, shut the fuck up, princess, and give me some sugar.

(HUNG *and* MOLLY *kiss. Lights fade...*)

5

QUI: So what do you think of the rewrite?

ABBY: ARE YOU FUCKING CRAZY????

QUI: You said for me to make it more like myself.

ABBY: You have aliens in it?

QUI: Yeah.

ABBY: You have aliens in your Gook Story Trilogy?

QUI: Yeah.

ABBY: That's fucking weird, Qui.
And you put me in your play?

QUI: Yeah, isn't that cool?

ABBY: Please don't put me in your play.

QUI: You said to make it more personal.

ABBY: I said to "have fun with it", not to completely wreck your story. Or throw yourself literally into the play as a side storyline. Or me. Or aliens. Or me.

QUI: Okay, so maybe the aliens were a bit too much.

ABBY: And what the fuck are you doing in your play?

QUI: You said I should be in it.

ABBY: As a character. Not as the literal playwright.

QUI: It's an artistic choice.

ABBY: It's someone else's artistic choice.

QUI: What do you mean?

ABBY: Didn't David Henry Hwang just do this? Like two years ago?

QUI: Yeah, but...it's not like he owns the device. No one probably even remembers...

ABBY: He got nominated for a Pulitzer for it. Hon, it's pretty clear that device has just been done. And quite well. Way better than the way you're using it.

QUI: Are you finished?

ABBY: And he's also David Henry Hwang, Qui. I love you, but you're not David Henry Hwang. People actually want to know what David Henry Hwang has to say about his Asian-ness. You've written like one play on the matter.

QUI: Two actually. TRIAL BY WATER and BLOOD IN AMERICA.

ABBY: BLOOD IN AMERICA has never even been produced.

QUI: Still counts.

ABBY: Fine. Okay. Two plays on the matter. And, also, it's all coming off as a little—

QUI: What?

ABBY: Pretentious.

QUI: You think I'm being pretentious?

ABBY: Why can't you just write the story the way you've always wanted to write it?

QUI: Who's to say this isn't the way I want to write it?

ABBY: Because you've told me this story a million times. I've heard you tell it to other people.

QUI: This story? I'm just now writing this story. How can I have possibly told it before.

ABBY: Not this one, Qui. The real story. Hung's actual story.

QUI: I already wrote a play about it.

ABBY: Did you?

QUI: Yeah, it was super Asian too. It even had Vietnamese in it.

ABBY: Qui—

QUI: Look, if you don't want to support me on this, then fine. But you don't have to make me feel bad about it, okay?

ABBY: Baby.

QUI: Whatever! I'll fix it!

6

HUNG: ...I killed your father. I'm so sorry.

SAN: Why, Hung? Why did you come here? Why?

(HUNG *cautiously approaches* SAN.)

HUNG: San.

SAN: I just wanted to be happy again. Like when I was small. Like before this all happened.

HUNG: I don't think I can give that to you.

SAN: God.

HUNG: But I'm willing to try.

SAN: You lie.

HUNG: I'll stay, San. I'll stay if that's what you want.

MOLLY: What?

HUNG: I did something horrible, San. I want to make up for that.

SAN: You'd stay?

HUNG: If that's what you want.

SAN: What about your wife?

MOLLY: Yeah, what about her?

HUNG: I think I have to do what's right, San. My passions brought me to this, they brought me to killing Tien. If my heart brought me to sin, then let my mind bring me to salvation.

(DAVID HENRY HWANG *enters. However this D H H is more like Dwayne "The Rock" Johnson than the actual playwright.*)

DAVID: Nice play, dick face!

QUI: Whoa! What the fuck? Now who are you supposed to be?

DAVID: I'm David Henry Hwang, motherfucker!

QUI: Wait, you're supposed to be David Henry Hwang?

DAVID: Well, you're supposed to be Qui Nguyen.

QUI: Touche'.

DAVID: As I said, I'm David Henry Hwang and you're in big trouble, Ass-Dick!

QUI: What? Are you here to sue me?

DAVID: No, Fuck-tard. I'm not here to sue you. What kind of Asian do you think I am. I'm here to kill you.

QUI: What?

DAVID: Who do you think keeps sending those fucking ninjas after your characters this whole time?
Putting yourself into your own play. Clearly, that is my device.

QUI: It's not your device. People have done it before. Have you never heard of Woody Allen? Or Kevin Smith?

DAVID: Yes, but none of them are yellow like you and me. I'm the trademark yella guy of this town. If you want to be Asian and do something remotely interesting, you have to go through me first.

QUI: That's stupid.

DAVID: Let me ask you something. How many other East Asian Playwrights have made it on Broadway?

QUI: Well...

DAVID: NONE! And as long as I'm here, I'm going to be the only splash of yellow on the great white way, do you hear me, DOWN TOWN playwright?

QUI: That's uncalled for.

DAVID: Am I hurting your feelings?

QUI: Fine. You wanna battle? Then let's battle.

DAVID: D J. Give me an old school beat! Time to school this bitch!

(Mics fall from the ceiling into QUI's *and* DAVID's *hands. A beat hits. The two rap battle.)*

DAVID: I'm the D double H
Playwright Master Hwang
Gonna kill ya with my lyrics
Gonna smash with this song

Ya wanna face me?
I'll destroy ya quickly
As I groove so freshly
Like a hip hop bruce lee

Cause I'm the unstoppable,
The total unbelievable,

My hunger's insatiable,
My hotness undeniable.
The thriller sensation
The king of all Asians
I reign devastation
On the whole population

I got Tonys and Obies,
And Pulitzer Prizes
Well, the last one's a nominee
But you still can't deny that

There'd still be yellowface if it weren't for me
Actually, there'd be no you if it weren't for me,
or Young Jean Lee or plays like B F E
You all owe me for anything that you be

So give it up now, though this has been fun—
Besides ripping me off, what the fuck have you done?

QUI: I paved the way for geek theater plays
Put sci-fi on the stage,
Made stage fights all the rage.
Made superheroes for the ethnics and the gays,
Got the crowds screaming yay
Got the geeks singing praise

ALL: New York & Brooklyn!

QUI: cheering all night
To all the stories I write
To all the fights that we fight

So no I might not be in no history books

For this play or that play or this show or that

But we made comic book theater before the big fad and
our heroes are original, so fuck Spider-Man

So legendary, yeah, you may be,
With your shiny-ass Tony and your sack of Obies

But the only peeps that created me
Are the geeks and the peeps of my theater V C

So keep on fuckin' hatin all you fuckin' want!
I'm Qui fuckin' Nguyen! Fuck you, Mister Hwang!

DAVID: Stop right there

Don't embarrass yo'self
You may know karate
But Imma black belt
You think you're spitting hot
But you're playing ya'self
You have coupla hits,
But my whole rep is def

Talking trash with garbage raps,
Here comes the heat
It's time to throwdown
With the number one chink!

I'm the D double H
Playwright Master Hwang
Gonna make you my bitch now
Like I did to Miss Saigon

(DAVID *smacks* QUI *to the ground.*)

DAVID: Ka-pow! *(Standing victorious)*
I am the greatest playwright eveeeer!!!!

QUI: Yeah, whatever.

DAVID: What was that?

QUI: I mean, "Yay, you win!" Look, I don't even wanna
be here. You wanna kick me outta my own play, be
my fucking guest. To tell you the truth, this shit's
uncomfortable.

DAVID: No, you wanna be here. You want to be the
next me.

QUI: No, I don't.

DAVID: Yes, you do.

QUI: No, I really really don't. I don't give a shit about Broadway or being Asian or whether or not I'm ever gonna be considered the next big yella sensation or not. I really don't. All I want to do right now is to just go home and forget all about this.

(HUNG *enters.*)

HUNG: But you can't.

QUI: What are you doing, Hung?

HUNG: You can't go home. Not til you finish it right.

QUI: No one cares if I get this "right".

HUNG: Yes, they do.

QUI: Who?

ALL: Us!

QUI: I can't.

HUNG: You haven't even tried.

QUI: You want to see what happens when I try? You want to see my attempt at telling something right? This is what happens.

SEXY WHITE GIRL: And now, you naughty boys and girls, an actual scene from TRIAL BY WATER, the first script in Qui Nguyen's A GOOK STORY TRILOGY.

HUNG: Wake up, Tien.

TIEN: What do you want?

HUNG: I want to talk now.

SAN: TRIAL BY WATER is really a trial by language. It clumsily imagines two tempest-tossed young boat people and their plight into the unknown. —*The New Yorker*

TIEN: Hey. Untie me.

HUNG: In Vietnam, I used to be a Buddhist.
I used to believe in things. Don't lie. Don't steal. Don't
kill.

MOLLY: The best of intentions do not necessarily
produce the best of plays. Such is the case with Qui
Nguyen's TRIAL BY WATER, a flawed piece indeed.
—*The Jewish Post & Observer*

HUNG: You killed my brother.

TIEN: No, I didn't.

SAN: It seems this story could only be told as a
tragedy. However, by oscillating between comedy and
melodrama, TRIAL BY WATER squanders the power
of its powerful story. —*The New York Sun*

HUNG: You lied.

MOLLY: Hung extracts a knife.

TIEN: What are you doing with that?

HUNG: I'm not in Vietnam anymore.

SAN: HUNG stabs TIEN.

TIEN: AAAAAAAAGH!

MOLLY: Qui Nguyen's tone-deaf new play TRIAL BY
WATER sinks almost as soon as it casts off, dragging
a promising premise along with it. Its cardboard
characters and muddled plot quickly find their way to
the bottom of the Sea of Plausibility. —*Newsday*

SAN: Some life experiences are so horrific that a
metaphorical language is needed to stage them.
However, the hectoring tone of Qui Nguyen's preachy
text makes this a heavy crossing. —*Variety*

MOLLY: Unfortunately, what could have been a drama
of survival and suffering turns into "Boat of the Living
Dead" in Nguyen's imagination. —*Backstage*

SAN: It was sad to see such talent wasted on such a horrible horrible play. —E-mail from an Angry Audience Member

MOLLY: It just made me sick to my stomach. —Qui's ex-girlfriend

TIEN: I didn't understand it. —Qui's Mom

SAN: I hate this play. —Me.

MOLLY: I hate this playwright. —Me

TIEN: Yeah, fuck this guy, someone should punch him in the cock. —Me

SAN: What a dick!

MOLLY: What a fucking asshole!

TIEN: Seriously, people actually fucking like this guy? What are they? Fucking geeks?

SAN: Fuck Qui Nguyen.

MOLLY: Yeah, fuck him!

(The actor playing TIEN *begins a "QUI NGUYEN SUCKS" chant. Slowly the rest of the cast begins chanting along. It rises in volume.)*

MOLLY, SAN & TIEN:
QUI NGUYEN SUCKS!
QUI NGUYEN SUCKS!
QUI NGUYEN SUCKS!
QUI NGUYEN—

(As it crescendos—)

HUNG: STOP!!! *(To* QUI*)* This a little unfair, don't you think?

QUI: Yeah, the press fucking destroyed me.

HUNG: That's not what I mean. I'm talking about what you're doing.

QUI: I'm not doing anything.

HUNG: You're only painting half the picture. You're giving a skewed version of reality.

QUI: Bullshit.

HUNG: Ahem...and I quote:

However beneath the shrieks and fake blood, Nguyen's play also asks an absorbing question no fifteen year-old should have to answer. —*The Village Voice*

QUI: That's not really a rave, now is it?

HUNG: Mr Nguyen raises questions that stay in the mind. —*The New York Times*

QUI: Yeah, that's not winning me any blowjobs either.

HUNG: Qui Nguyen's new play is brilliant. So powerful it leaves its audience as changed as the main character himself. —*Show Business Weekly*

QUI: Hung, stop.

HUNG: This is tour-de-force theater. —*Timeout New York*
A beautifully written script! —*Newcity Chicago*
Should I go on?

QUI: It doesn't matter.

HUNG: Why? Because it stops you and your pity party?

QUI: No. Because what you're reading is bullshit. They have it wrong.
The ones who said I fucked it all up. They're right.

HUNG: Qui.

QUI: All I ever wanted to do was to tell my family's story. To tell it the way it actually happened. But all I ever got was notes. Notes on how it could be more dramatic. Notes on how it should be structured and told and rewritten. The two boys are too young to be cast-able. We need more of a reason for them to be on the ship. We need an antagonist. "This story cries for an antagonist!" And I wrote it the way I was told to write it to make it more produce-able, more marketable, more "right for the medium of theatre". And it's wrong. It's not the story. There's no truth in it. There never was. It was broken the minute I decided making a "good play" was more important than making a truthful one.

HUNG: Then what is the story, Qui?

QUI: It's too long.

HUNG: This is your opportunity, playwright. Tell it.

QUI: There's no arc. No character development. No structure.

HUNG: Do it your way.

QUI: It's too long of a story, no one will listen—

HUNG: You might be surprised.

QUI: It paints Vietnamese in a bad light.

HUNG: Who cares?

QUI: I care.

(HUNG *grabs a mic and mic-stand and places it in the middle of the stage.*)

HUNG: Tell. It.

(*The rest of the cast leaves* QUI *onstage alone in a single spotlight.*)

7

QUI: This is retarded, guys. Seriously. I don't know how...

Hey! HEY! Goddammit. (*He looks at the mic stand and slowly approaches it.*) Fine. "Do it my way". Okay. Okay.

QUI: Here it goes. *(He starts trying to free-style a poem
slowly.)*
Forget all the words
That occurred
before this moment
So this
is the real shit
behind this fiction
I had written
about my cousin
who lost everything

Erase from your brain
these sights
Hung's no killer super-spy
Both Tien and San are both lies
Even his girlfriend here is a lie

So check this
I writ this
So you could witness
the tragic
story
that befell and hit this
Nine year old boy named Hung
And his parents who did all they could
to ensure their kids would live free
even if it meant they'd die out at sea

I tried so hard to tell it right
Gimme one last chance here tonight

He didn't give-up
Didn't die
No matter what came
He survived
he was just a boy
only nine

Lost his entire world
but not his life

(As QUI *begins building momentum and flow, he signals to
the booth for a beat to drop. The rest of the poem becomes a
rap/song.*)

QUI: *(Rapping)*
Late
on the date
of May 88
they made their escape
to reshape their fate
taking destiny in hand
Used all the money they had
to leave Vietnam
to find freedom

Crammed on a boat so tight
with a hundred and ten taking flight
After two days in
their engine gives in
leaving them stranded
in the middle of the ocean

Then they started to run out of food
Hung's father does what fathers do
Gave all his rations up to
his boys to help them live through

But after two weeks
without drop to drink
or a damn thing to eat
or any land to seek
His father closes his eyes
tells his boys a final good-bye

QUI: *(Singing)*
But Hung didn't give-up
Didn't die
No matter what came

He survived
he was just a boy
only nine
Lost his entire world
but not his life

(Rapping)
One week later was his mom
Died with her sons asleep in her arms
Gave all the food that she had
In hopes to help them both last

But his big bro who was my age
Just eleven when he met his fate
fainted and fell off the side
Got swept away out of sight

His death makes a heart hurt
He had yet to even kiss a girl
He was just a boy, not a man
A future gone for freedom

It was here when the ship went crazy
A group of madmen began to slay the
weaker passengers to sate the
hunger pangs of their cravings

QUI: *(Singing)*
He didn't give-up
Didn't die
No matter what came
He survived
he was just a boy
only nine
Lost his entire world
but not his life

QUI: *(Rapping)*
After thirty-six days they were found
Only fifty-two made it out
Three months later

he came to live with me
Our grandma sank to her knees

Alone
in our home
he spoke of his soul
his heart an empty hole
his life lost control
We promised we would help him
Do all we could to heal him
as long as there was breath
we would always be there for him

Eleven years later our grandma died
I promised Hung's story be the first thing I'd write
I promised that promise the first day of my
playwright M F A, but couldn't write it right

Gave up everything
to be free
Watched the sea
take his family
I just wanted to tell his story
But I failed,
Please forgive me

QUI: *(Singing)*
He didn't give-up
Didn't die
No matter what came
He survived

He was just a boy
only nine
Lost his entire world
but not his life

He didn't give-up
Didn't die
No matter what came
He survived

He was just a boy
only nine

Lost his entire world
but not his life
He didn't give-up
Didn't die
No matter what came
He survived
He was just a boy
only nine

Lost his entire world
but not his life

(HUNG *steps out from the shadows. The two boys lock eyes.*)

QUI: So?

HUNG: It's a start.

(Fade to black...)

END OF PLAY